AFTER SCHOOL

School Band

Kristine Hooks

HIGH
interest
books

Children's Press
A Division of Scholastic Inc.
New York / Toronto / London / Auckland / Sydney
Mexico City / New Delhi / Hong Kong
Danbury, Connecticut

Thanks to the Upper Darby High School, Upper Darby, PA

Book Design: Michelle Innes
Contributing Editor: Matthew Pitt
Photo Credits: Cover (right side), pp. 1, 32–39 by Maura Boruchow; cover (left side), pp. 3–4, 6, 8, 13, 16–17, 23 (background), 25, 29, 30 (top), 31 © Photodisc; pp. 5, 16, 18, 22, © AP/Wide World Photos; pp. 7, 15, 21, 23 (top) 27, 30 (bottom), 40–41 © Corbis; p. 24 © FPG International

Visit Children's Press on the Internet at:
http://publishing.grolier.com

Library of Congress Cataloging-in-Publication Data

Hooks, Kristine.
    School Band / Kristine Hooks.
        p. cm. -- (After school)
    Includes bibliographical references (p.) and index.
    ISBN 0-516-23153-7 (lib. bdg.) -- ISBN 0-516-29557-8 (pbk.)
    1. Bands (Music)--Juvenile literature. [1. Bands (Music) 2. Musical Instruments.] I. Title. II. Series.

ML1300 .H66 2001
784.4'4--dc21   2001017485

CONTENTS

INTRODUCTION

Are you a music fan looking to make noise? Join the school band! Band is a very popular extracurricular activity. Extracurricular activities are things you do after school. Most students join school bands because they love playing music. It's also an easy way to make new friends.

You and your bandmates will have to work hard. The work pays off, though. When you win a competition or hear cheers from a smiling audience, you'll be glad you chose band. This book will march you through the steps. You'll learn about different types of band programs. We'll give you tips on auditions, competitions, and practices. This book even helps you choose the perfect instrument!

Performing in parades is one of the highlights of being in a school band.

CHAPTER ONE

Life in a School Band

MUSIC TO THE EARS

Reading music is like learning a foreign language or putting a puzzle together. The more you practice, the more you learn to concentrate. Being able to concentrate will help you in other areas of school, such as studying for tests. If your math scores go up without doing more homework, that really is a big benefit!

Another benefit of participating in your school's music program is that you will become more cultured. Right now you may only listen to hip-hop or rock. When you're in the school band, you begin to learn about marches, symphonies, and jazz. The more kinds of music you know, the easier it is to express your creativity.

Learning to read music can help free your creativity. It can also improve your ability to concentrate and study.

Being in a school band keeps you busy throughout the year. Some days, you'll rehearse new songs for upcoming performances. Other times, you may work on familiar pieces of music for a holiday concert. Most bands compete and perform concerts about the same time each year.

Your band experience depends on the kind of program you join. Some schools offer several

playing new music

Playing new music for the first time can often be a challenge. It's like reading a difficult book for the first time. You might stumble over the words. You probably won't recognize the most important parts. But if you practice reading the book over and over, you will pick things up. Then, your reading will have more nuance, or expression.

different programs, including concert band, marching band, jazz band, and orchestra.

Joining band usually means you will take music class as an elective. An elective is a class that is not required. It's a class you choose to take because it matches your personal skills and interests. Other types of electives include art, drama, and debate. Electives often are connected with after-school activities. Art students exhibit drawings and sculptures at art shows. Drama students perform in plays after school. Band members go to music class during school hours. After school, they rehearse for performances and competitions.

Classroom Instruction

Each semester, your music teacher will introduce several new pieces of music. You begin to learn each new song by "reading" through it in class. This is called a first run-through. The piece probably won't sound very good right away. You shouldn't be worried if you make mistakes when you first learn a new song. Practices will perfect the new music.

After your first read-through, your conductor or director will teach the music in smaller parts. You might practice the song's introduction first, with instructions on how to play that part. Perhaps the part is played slowly with a deep, heavy sound. Maybe it's played lightly and quickly.

Directors often use class time to work with different sections of the band. For example, the director might ask the brass section to play the song alone. Then he or she might ask the woodwind section to do the same. Sometimes, the director even may ask each woodwind instrument to play its part alone—first the flutes, then the clarinets, and then the oboes. Directors make sure that each player plays the right notes. They also listen to the players, making sure that they play at the right speed, or tempo. These are the technical parts of the song, and they must be learned first.

If you listen to what the director tells the other sections, it can help you understand the music better. Many people use the time when they aren't playing to practice the finger positions for each note. These positions are known as fingerings. This is a way to practice without actually playing notes.

After you learn the song's technical parts, you start playing it all the way through. This

You don't have to make sounds to learn music! Players can practice their fingering positions quietly.

takes time. The director probably will stop often to ask the whole band or individual sections to try things differently. He or she might ask the brass section to play more softly or the percussion section to play more clearly. During these rehearsals, you will be developing the style and feeling of the song.

Marching band members can't carry music sheets while they perform. They must memorize the songs, or learn them by heart. This is not as hard as it sounds. Even when you don't have to memorize a song, you'll practice it so many times that you'll probably know it by heart anyway.

Marching Band Practices

What you do during practice depends on what you're practicing for. If you're practicing for a concert, then after-school practices will be much the same as in-class rehearsals. Practices for marching band performances are quite different.

At a competition, judges check to see that all marchers move smoothly. That means you must walk as if you were balancing books on your head. This is easy if you practice the "roll" step. First, step forward with your left foot leading. Let your left heel gently hit the ground. Roll the left foot toward the toes. Begin to bring your right foot up. Then, land on your right heel. Finally, roll your right foot from heel to toe. This roll step will help keep your head steady. And that will turn the judges' heads!

Marching band performances involve playing music while moving around the football field in different formations. The simplest formation calls for everyone to make a straight line. The band then takes each step together, or in unison. Your director probably will make up complicated formations. Lines of people may move across the field to form shapes and patterns, including squares and letters.

Rehearsals usually start late in the summer. The director tells everyone where to line up on the field. Then he or she gives you and your linemates directions where to move. The director also tells you how many steps you'll take to get there, and how many beats to wait before moving again. At first, you'll practice these steps without playing your instrument.

Moving into different formations is challenging. The audience is going to be watching from the stadium seats. If your line is crooked,

A well-trained band is often a hit at the half-time show.

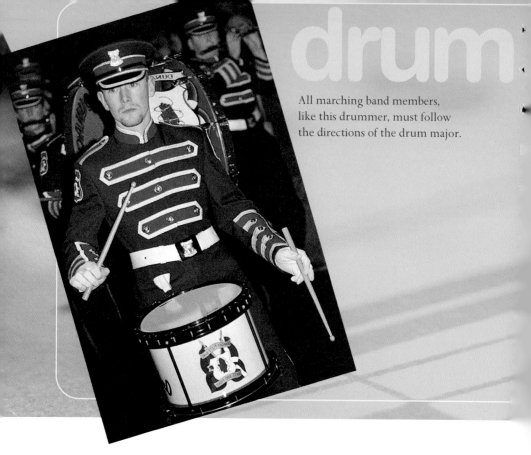

All marching band members, like this drummer, must follow the directions of the drum major.

the audience will see it. It's very important to learn to "hit your marks!" That means getting to your assigned spot for every formation. It's even more important to make sure you're lining up in sync with the people next to you.

In some formations, you need to be a step ahead of the person beside you. This way, you can form a curve. There's a trick to this, though. You cannot move your head from side to side to check where you're lined up. You

major

Before the marching band season starts, there probably will be an audition for the position of drum major. The drum major conducts the band while band members perform on the field. He or she takes an active role in leading practices and rehearsals. Other band members are expected to follow the drum major's directions. If you have strong music and leadership skills, you should definitely try out for this position.

have to use your peripheral vision, which means checking out of the corners of your eyes.

After you rehearse the formations, it's time to add the instruments. It isn't easy to walk around a football field in different directions while playing an instrument! But practice makes perfect. Your director will instruct you to practice each formation over and over, until you can almost sleepwalk your way through the performance.

Taking private lessons is a good way to perfect new songs.

Practices will become more complex as you learn the moves and add the instruments. You'll have to remember to stay in sync, hit your marks, play softer in some parts, and get ready for the big finale—all at the same time! It can be tough work, but keep at it. It's going to pay off at performance time!

Practicing at Home

You learn a lot at rehearsals. But practicing on your own time is just as important. You can rehearse music either by yourself or during lessons with a private instructor.

Not every band student takes private lessons. If you do sign up for them, you'll probably go to your teacher once a week. You'll practice drills that the teacher has assigned. Private instructors help develop your musical skills. They also help you perfect new songs.

If you're interested in private lessons, ask your director for help. You might want to meet several instructors before deciding. Don't be afraid to ask questions. Find out how many years they've been teaching and what kind of preparation they expect. Ask your parents to come along. They may have questions, too.

Even if you don't take private lessons, you definitely should practice at home. First, play the scales to get your fingers and mouth warmed up. (Unless you're a percussionist. They warm up with basic rhythm drills.) After warming up, start practicing your parts in the songs. Practice the harder parts slowly at first, then build up to the normal speed. You also can use your own practice time to memorize music. A good rule of thumb is to practice for 30 minutes a day, every day!

Time to Shine

Finally, after all the practice, you get to the payoff—performances and competitions. During the fall, the marching band performs at half-time shows for football games. The band also plays lively marches and the school's fight songs while seated in the bleachers. These performances let you show a live audience how hard you've worked. They give you and your bandmates a great sense of camaraderie, or friendship. You get to express your school spirit and hear the roar of the crowd. The best part is that you do these things with dozens of your closest friends!

At football games and pep rallies, the marching band gets to strut its stuff.

Concerts are also very rewarding. Sitting onstage in your school's auditorium, you will be dressed for a fancy event. You'll perform beautiful music for your family and friends. The standing ovation at the end of the concert can really lift you up.

Your band probably also will enter local competitions. There, you'll meet other school bands from the area. In front of a panel of judges, you'll perform songs you've been practicing. At the end of the day, the judges add up scores from all the schools and name winners in different categories. Some categories include best all-around, best percussion section, and best woodwind section.

These band members show off their new trophy.

Music programs often have a hard time getting funding. There isn't always enough money to send your band on trips. That's where you get involved! School bands have fundraisers throughout the year. Your bandmates might sell magazine subscriptions door to door or host a car wash at a gas station.

fundraisers

This school band is about to head off on a weekend trip.

If the competition is far away, it might be time to load up the school bus and take a trip. Bus trips can provide some really fun band memories. If you stay overnight for a competition, you can explore a new town with your friends. Then you'll have an exciting adventure to tell your family about!

CHAPTER TWO

Getting Started

JOINING UP

Most people who join a school band already have some experience playing an instrument. Those people probably won't have trouble getting started. But even if you've never picked up an instrument before, it's not too late to start learning to play.

Before you join, discuss your choice with your parents. They will want to know the details. Ask the band director to give information to your parents. Try to tell your parents how much time you'll have to devote to band, and how much it will cost. Do you have to buy or rent an instrument or can you borrow one? Do you have to pay for your uniform?

Choosing Your Program

As you read in Chapter One, some schools have just one band. It's a marching band during the fall and a concert band during the spring. But if your school offers other choices, you might consider them, too. The type of instrument you want to play also may influence your decision. For instance, marching and concert bands usually don't have a string section. If you want to play the violin, viola, or cello, join your school orchestra. The orchestra consists mostly of string instruments.

Your school also might offer a jazz band. This is smaller than a concert band or orchestra. It usually includes guitars, percussion, a piano, and brass and woodwind instruments. If you love music but do not play an instrument, you might think about joining the school choir.

Auditioning

Depending on how many people want to be in the band, you might have to audition. Even if everyone is guaranteed a spot, there usually is an audition to rank the players in "chairs." Your rank determines where you sit. For example, the clarinet player with the best audition is ranked first chair. The player with the second-best audition is second chair. These rankings also determine who performs the solos for the instruments.

A cellist prepares to compete for first chair.

Usually an audition takes place at the beginning of the year to determine chairs. Your director may schedule other auditions throughout the year. This gives everyone a chance to move up. It also encourages ambitious players to practice hard.

In an audition, you sometimes are alone with the judge. Other times, you're with other students who play your instrument. While judging, your band director might sit behind a screen or with his or her back to the players. Everyone who auditions is assigned a number. The director starts out by saying, "Player Number 1, please play a C scale." As called, each player performs a few different scales. Players also have an opportunity to play a prepared piece. You might be asked to play a piece without having practiced it. This is called sight reading. The judge awards points for good technique, musical ability, expression, and sight reading. After the points are added up, the judge announces the order of players.

If you're one of the top players in your band, the director might ask you to try out for a regional band. To join a regional band, you will audition and compete against other top players in the area. If you're selected, you probably will attend rehearsals during a school break. At the end of a three-day rehearsal process, the regional band performs a recital. The best regional players may be invited to audition for state and national competitions!

If you don't make the position you wanted at first, practice, practice, practice even harder. Try to move ahead the next time!

Some school bands may have only male trumpet players. Others may have only female flute players. But there are absolutely no rules about girls playing one kind of instrument and boys playing another. Try several different instruments before choosing. Pick the one you like best.

CHAPTER THREE

Choosing an Instrument

Before joining a band, it's important to know which instrument you want to play. This chapter gives an overview of the major types of instruments.

The lists in this chapter do not even begin to cover all the different types. Talk to your band director about other options. The director may not be able to make room for a ukulele, an accordion, or the bagpipes. But maybe he or she can suggest a local group who shares your passion for that instrument.

Woodwinds, brass instruments, percussion and strings are some instrument groups that you typically will find in a school band or orchestra.

It's important to pick an instrument that interests you.

Woodwinds

Flutes, clarinets, oboes, and saxophones are examples of woodwinds. Woodwind instruments traditionally were made from long, straight pieces of hollowed wood. Flutes now are almost always made of metal. Saxophones are made of brass. A woodwind instrument produces noise when air is blown through the instrument's body. Covering some holes in the body and leaving others open allow different notes to be played.

Some woodwinds also are known as reed instruments. Clarinets and saxophones are single-reed instruments. Oboes are double-reeds. As you blow through the mouthpiece, the reeds vibrate. The instrument's tone changes with the amount of air blown into it. Touching the tongue lightly to the reed also changes the sound.

These band members practice playing woodwind instruments.

Brass Instruments

These include trumpets, tubas, and French horns. As the name suggests, these instruments are made of tubes of twisted brass. Sound is made by blowing air through the instrument. Air travels through the tubing and vibrates on the brass as it moves along. Pressing and releasing valves in the instrument create different notes. Except for the trombone, all brass instruments have air valves you push with your fingers. Trombones have a slide valve that is moved in and out.

Brass instruments are much louder than woodwinds. Sometimes, brass players have to put a device inside the mouthpiece to muffle the sound. That device is called a mute.

Brass instruments include the French horn and the trumpet.

Percussion

When people talk about percussion, they usually mean drums. But a percussion instrument can be anything that you tap or strike to make a noise. Some specific types include the snare drum, the bass drum, the tympani, the xylophone, the cymbals, and the triangle. Hitting or tapping a drumstick, mallet, or brush on different parts of percussion instruments creates the sounds.

Unlike the other sections, most instruments in the percussion section don't play musical notes. Most percussionists instead play rhythms that form a base for the songs.

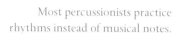

Most percussionists practice rhythms instead of musical notes.

Strings

As you read earlier, string instruments such as the violin, viola, and cello are not part of a marching band. But they are the main part of an orchestra. String instruments can produce many tones. When played well, these instruments can sound like beautiful singing.

Running a bow over the strings produces sounds. A bow is a long stick made of fine strands strung tightly together. Depending on where it strikes, the bow produces different musical notes. String players also press their fingers against the strings to increase and decrease the amount of tension. All of this activity causes vibrations that can lead to beautiful music.

If you are interested in string instruments, you should audition for the orchestra.

No matter which instrument or music group you choose, you will experience the value of hard work in school band. You will learn to master pieces of music, and perform them for judges, students, and parents. The best part is that you won't do the hard work alone. You'll be joined by many other dedicated musicians who help make the hours of practice seem like the best time in the world!

When you join a school band, you make great friends and great music!

NEW WORDS

camaraderie a feeling of great friendship or closeness

elective a class you choose to take

extracurricular in addition to regular school courses

fingerings practicing where your fingers move for each note

formation the arrangement of a marching band into a shape or a pattern

linemates the marching band members in your formation

memorize to learn by heart

NEW WORDS

nuance a subtle quality of feeling and expression

ovation when an audience cheers for a performance

peripheral out of the corner of your eye

scales a series of musical tones going up or down in pitch

tempo the speed at which a song is played

unison everyone moving at the same time

FOR FURTHER READING

Ardley, Neil. *Eyewitness: Music.* New York: Dorling Kindersley, 2000.

Ardley, Neil. *Young Person's Guide to Music.* New York: Dorling Kindersley, 1995.

O'Brien, Eileen. *The Usborne Story of Music.* Tulsa: EDC Publications, 1998.

Nathan, Amy. *The Young Musician's Survival Guide: Tips from Teens and Pros.* New York: Oxford University Press, 2000.

RESOURCES

Associations

Youth Education in the Arts
http://yea.org
P.O. Box 506
198 N. Washington Ave.
Bergenfield, NJ 07621
(201) 384-8822

The National Association for Music Education
http://menc.org
1806 Robert Fulton Drive
Reston, VA 20191
(703) 860-4000

RESOURCES

Bandfest

http://bandfest.com

This site provides information about scholar-ships for young musicians. There are also links to the Web sites of high school bands across the United States.

VH-1

http://vh1.com

This "Save the Music" site helps bands who need funding support.

Pepsi

http://www.pepsinotes.com

This site for the "Pepsi Notes" program pro-vides a way for school bands to raise money.

INDEX

INDEX

About the Author
Kristine Hooks is a lawyer living in New York City. She played the clarinet in her high school marching band and won several regional and state championships.